HYBRID LEARNING ENVIRONMENTS: WHAT, WHY, AND HOW

EFFECTIVELY TEACH BY MERGING IN-PERSON LEARNING ENVIRONMENTS WITH ONLINE LEARNING ENVIRONMENTS

MELANIE WELLS

First Printing, 2020

Print ISBN 978-1-7357124-0-6
Ebook ISBN 978-1-7357124-1-3

Printed in the United States of America

115 Metroplex Blvd
Pearl, MS 39208
agpearl.com

DEDICATION

This book is dedicated to Josie L. Wells, Sr., my A-1 since day one. "Thank God for the memories we had when we were growing up." Jo, this one is for you.

FOREWORD

By Dr. Denver J. Fowler

"A must-read for educators who want to learn how to effectively utilize hybrid learning environments for teaching and learning."

In the 21st Century, it has become apparent that hybrid learning can effectively take place both in the PK-12 educational setting and higher education setting, namely as it applies to teaching and learning. More recently, due to the COVID-19 pandemic, it has forced numerous educators and professors to re-think how they might approach 100% remote or hybrid modalities of course design and instruction. Thus, Wells' book is most certainly a timely addition to the extant literature on remote learning modalities, be it 100% remote or hybrid. In *Hybrid Learning Environments: What, Why, and How,* Wells clearly reviews the "what," "why," and "how" of the hybrid learning environment. In addition, Wells makes a strong case for why educators should shift to the hybrid approach. In addition to real-life scenarios and examples shared throughout the book, Wells connects numerous theories (e.g., Piaget, Bloom, Maslow, etc.) to the idea of hybrid learning environments, and thoroughly reviews numerous aspects that apply to this modality, including effective teaching styles and the flipped classroom model. Another facet of the book that shines is the focus on optimal learning environments. Here Wells provides the reader with sound advice as to ensuring the learning environment is optimal regardless of the fact that it is online or hybrid versus face-to-face. It is here, in this section of the book, that Wells provides key information on active engagement, sample hybrid learning lesson planning (including the design of assignments & assessments), textbook selection, the merging of teaching styles, and how to monitor student progress – essentially painting a clear picture for the reader of what a hybrid learning class looks like. Wells' book is a must-read for educators who want to learn how to effectively utilize hybrid learning environments for teaching and learning. With almost (if not all) colleges and universities utilizing online and hybrid versions of their programs and courses in addition to their face-to-face options, the content of this book will most surely support the goal of ensuring our students in PK-12 are college, career, and life ready upon graduation.

Dr. Denver J. Fowler is an Associate Professor of Educational Leadership & Policy Studies at Southern Connecticut State University in New Haven, Connecticut.

ACKNOWLEDGEMENTS

First, giving honor to God for His grace and favor. I am beyond amazed at His talents and creativeness. God is "Alpha and Omega, the Beginning and the End." The first circular pattern revealed to me- a circle radiating love, faith, and hope.

I want to thank my parents, Obie and Sherry Wells, Sr., and my siblings for supporting me during this process. Their love, strength, guidance, and support are immeasurable and invaluable. As a family, I pray we continue to always know "the power of love."

I would also like to thank my grandparents and family members who came before me. I am forever grateful for the great shoulders on which I stand. One of our daily Bible verses passed down and recited for generations is, "May the Lord watch between me and thee while we are absent one from another." Genesis 31:49 serves as a gentle reminder of the love of a strong family.

I thank my family, friends, cover designer, and editors for showing their love, talents, and support. Lastly, I thank every student who was curious enough to ask, "When are we ever going to use this?"

HYBRID LEARNING ENVIRONMENTS: WHAT, WHY, and HOW

TABLE OF CONTENTS

HYBRID LEARNING ENVIRONMENTS: WHAT, WHY, AND HOW

Introduction- In the Blink of an Eye

"Change will not come if we wait for some other person or if we wait for some other time. We are the one we've been waiting for. We are the change that we seek."
~Barack Obama, 44th U.S. president

Take a sheet of paper and make a list of bugs. Be sure you step out of your comfort zone and think outside the box. (P.S. Do not look at some of the answers listed below).

Welcome back! I am sure you have an extensive list of bugs. See if your list contains any of the following:

A cold or stomach bug
A computer bug (virus)
Gummy worms
Bugs Bunny
Volkswagen Beetle
Beetlejuice
Bugs (wire and other listening devices to eavesdrop)

The above is an example of a lateral thinking activator. Lateral thinking activities encourage individuals to view problems from a different and creative angle. As educators, we must be willing to step out of our comfort zones to each our students' learning zones. Simple activities like this one promote growth mindsets by helping students put on their thinking caps. Growth mindset activities can easily be incorporated in hybrid learning environments as students open their minds to learning.

Think back to the start of the Coronavirus Disease 2019 (COVID-19) pandemic. What were you doing? How did you feel? Personally, I was excited because I was getting extra time to rest and relax, or so I thought. Reality hit and I realized this "extra" time would not be relaxing at all. In fact, it was hectic and a bit frightening. In the blink of an eye, our lives changed drastically. Education was shifting quickly without any strategic plans or directions. I was not worried about our students' learning gaps; after all, we are educators and can remediate them. I was worried about our students' mental and emotional health. Our students have spent months away from their teachers, classmates, and friends. Their routines were being affected, and some of our students lost their safety net. Like many others, I wondered how we could continue being the anchor in their lives.

I have been in education for 15 years. I have watched new initiatives, standardized testing formats, and multiple teaching programs filter in and out of our classrooms. Now more than ever, we need techniques that work. Educators need to be able to help our students navigate this new educational pathway successfully. Sometimes change comes naturally; sometimes we are forced to change. In the spring of 2020, COVID-19 forced educators to teach in unknown settings. Nervous and unsure we dove in headfirst, not because we wanted to, not because we had no fear, but because our students needed us. We spent hours thinking outside the box in order to continue meeting the needs of our students. It was a challenge for teachers, students, and parents; however, by joining forces, we successfully finished the school year.

Likewise, this upcoming school year will be new territory for everyone. This book will help educators learn how to merge effective in-person or "face-to-face" learning environments with effective online learning environments to create an effective hybrid learning experience. This newly created environment will increase student motivation, engagement, and academic achievement by encouraging students to learn in a safe and secure learning environment. According to author and researcher Eric Jenson, some children do not perform well at school because they live in a constant state of *fight or flight* survival mode (*Teaching with Poverty in Mind,* 2009). Hybrid learning environments allow students to relax and focus on learning instead of problematic situations that may be going on in their lives.

One year when I was teaching math, I had a student in my inclusion class who started off the year skipping my class. After three days of marking him absent, I asked my counselors for help. We soon realized he was going to every class except mine. The next day we made sure he came to my class. I introduced myself and showed him his seat. He sat on the edge of the seat as if he was ready to get up and run away. He was officially in my seventh-grade math class. After watching his behavior patterns over the next few days, I realized the problem. He was scared to come to math class because he felt like he did not belong. He did not think math was for him. He struggled in previous years, so what would make this year any different? He simply decided he was not going to give it a try. Daily, I devoted time to make sure he was in his optimal learning environment. I intentionally placed him with group members who would encourage him to learn. I called on him more during class discussions so he could share his thoughts and opinions. By the end of the year, he was smiling because he knew his value. His test scores increased because he was open to learning. On paper, he belonged in a special education classroom; however, what he really needed was to "belong" in a special classroom. By being in a special environment, he was able to use his strengths to find his worth, while defeating his weaknesses. Student engagement draws students' attention away from problems and insecurities. One of the best things we can do as educators is create a safe and secure learning environment to ease our students' minds. Learning occurs when students do not have to worry about social and emotional stress factors they may experience at home. Simon Sinek is an author and well-known public speaker among business and educational leaders around the world. His book *Start with Why: How Great Leaders Inspire Everyone to Take Action* centers on the importance of having a growth mindset and knowing one's purpose (Sinek, 2019). Students perform better when they feel valued by others and have a sense of purpose.

My book on hybrid learning environments will explain three educational theories: Maslow's *Hierarchy of Needs* (1943), Piaget's *Theory of Cognitive Development* (1936), and Bloom's *Taxonomy of Cognitive Skills* (1956). Most, if not all, of these theories are studied in undergraduate educational college courses. These models are traditionally seen in vertical form. However, these models should be viewed as a circular pattern constantly cycling from one level to the next. We will explore these circular patterns and discuss how they can be used to encourage a growth mindset, active engagement, and intrinsic motivation. This book will guide educators as they learn the what, why, and how of hybrid learning environments. It will also provide examples of activities and sample lesson plans to use when creating hybrid learning lessons. My goal for writing this book is to help teachers accomplish their goal of engaging and motivating students in any environment.

CHAPTER 1
HYBRID LEARNING ENVIRONMENTS
PASSION OVER FEAR

"Education is the most powerful weapon we can use to change the world."
~Nelson Mandela

What is Hybrid Learning?

Hybrid learning is not a new concept. It is used at most institutions of higher learning. Teachers often use hybrid learning, also known as blended learning, as a teaching method because it incorporates multiple teaching styles. These two versions of hybrid learning are not the same as *hybrid learning environments*. Hybrid learning environments refer to the merging of in-person and online learning. A database search of "hybrid learning" populates results relating to the hybrid and blended learning teaching methods mentioned above. In a hybrid learning environment, online assignments are not seen as add-ons. Instead, an online lesson is a different version of a structured lesson that is created for digital teaching and learning. It contains the same content as an in-person lesson. When a full and completed online lesson merges with a full and completed in-person lesson, they create a hybrid learning lesson that can be taught in any environment, hence the phrase *hybrid*. In this book, hybrid learning will refer to a lesson that can be taught both in-person and online.

Whether online or face-to-face, our first aim should be to ensure students are safe and motivated to learn. A hybrid learning environment is the perfect place for safe explorations and active engagement. Hybrid learning environments allow teachers to continue being effective by submerging students in in-depth content explorations. Due to time constraints, teachers sometimes feel like they have to skim the surface of many concepts as quickly as possible. Hybrid learning environments allow educational explorations that cover multiple concepts, which may be glossed over in traditional classroom setups due to limited time. Additionally, hybrid lessons permit teachers to take the best of both worlds and merge them together.

Why is it Important to Shift to Hybrid Learning Environments?

Have you ever had an item you cared about but rarely used because it was important to you? For me, it was a 3D television (3D TV). I did not use my 3D glasses regularly because I wanted to use them for special occasions. As it turned out, companies realized the 3D glasses were too expensive to replace. As a result, 3D TVs were phased out because they were not worth the hassle of repairing and replacing. At the time, I did not know 3D TVs were going to be obsolete and the next generation would replace it. Although I felt like I wasted my money, the replacement TV had more efficient attributes and features than my 3D TV. This same concept applies in education. The learning platform may change, but the purpose should remain the same. We have to shift in order to keep up with advancements in education and technology. The first step to shifting to hybrid is understanding why it is important to transition to hybrid learning environments.

Take a moment to consider business owners and their employees. A business owner should not have to constantly tell someone what to do. Most employers are seeking employees who complement their talents and bring new ideas to the table. If an employee cannot contribute positive and innovative ideas, that employee may no longer be needed. Another reason educational change is significant is some businesses wonder why they cannot retain their best employees. Employers are often tempted to change their routines. For example, some employers are considering flexible seating and "brain breaks" for their employees. Brain breaks are a relatively new concept being considered to maintain interest and motivation. According to researcher Mark Emmons, millennials crave engagement in their careers (Emmons, 2018). Employers probably do not experience a lack of motivation in their veteran employees because these workers understand the importance of stability and security. According to Emmons, most young adults feel safe to take risks as they select environments conducive to their talents. Many of them realize the importance of working in an enjoyable environment where they can unveil their passion and skills (Emmons, 2018). Understandably, our students crave this same environment while at school and at home. Educators can use hybrid learning environments to allow students to embrace and unveil their intellectual gifts.

How Can We Use Hybrid Learning to Motivate Students?

One way to develop intrinsic motivation is by sparking curiosity. Our brains naturally love a challenge. A few years ago, I bought my nephews small Lego packets. My eight-year-old nephew struggled to connect the Legos. He understood what was supposed to happen and even knew the steps; however, he could not piece the puzzle together. Frustrated, he hit the Legos, causing them to scatter. I helped him search for them, and I started to help him complete the puzzle when he said, "I can do it myself." I had an *Aha* moment because I felt like I needed to jump in and assist, but he did not need me to do the work for him. He needed me to encourage and guide him. When teaching, we may feel the need to tell students what to do; however, when we allow students to engage in productive struggles, we empower them to gain intrinsic motivation and discover their own understanding.

A teacher's mission should be to help students become intrinsically motivated to find and enhance their strengths. This motivation comes when students have a sense of purpose and worth. Some students do not know the purpose of education because they do not know their purpose *in* education. Students tend to admire visibly talented role models, such as musicians, athletes, and entertainers. We must help our students embrace their hidden and visible talents. When students do not know their value, they may struggle to see their role in the classroom. Students should be able to share their strengths with their peers. As students put forth the dedication needed to complete tasks, they will feel a sense of intrinsic motivation and self-worth. Our focal points in the following chapters will be teaching styles, educational theories, optimal learning environments, and hybrid learning lessons. Join me as we explore hybrid learning methods that inspire students to *win from within*.

NOTES

CHAPTER 2
EFFECTIVE TEACHING STYLES

"Mystery creates wonder and wonder is the basis of one's desire to understand."
~ Neil Armstrong

As a tutor for teacher candidates, I use a mixture of teaching styles in hybrid learning settings to prepare my participants for the standardized tests required in order to obtain their teacher certification. For example, I give my participants links to PowerPoints and videos to watch before our next meeting. When we come back together as a whole group, I can quickly clarify misconceptions and save time by not having to reteach lower-level skills. I also allow my participants to move around and explore concepts presented in conceptual development and inquiry-based formats. This flipped classroom setup enables me to incorporate various teaching styles as I use Bloom's Taxonomy to deepen knowledge acquisition. Certain teaching styles are highly effective when applied at various points in hybrid learning lessons.

Direct instruction involves the teacher presenting information to students in a direct way. This style of teaching usually involves instructors standing at the board or the front of the room. Sometimes learning is hindered because students are less likely to pay attention if they are not actively engaged. Although direct instruction may be considered old fashioned because students have access to the same information via the internet and other resources, it is still a useful teaching style. Direct instruction allows teachers to clarify misconceptions and highlight essential concepts needed to complete an interactive assignment or task. However, it may not be an effective teaching style when used to begin a lesson because direct instruction usually does not involve an engaging activity to motivate students.

As discussed earlier, we want to spark curiosity. This can be achieved with conceptual development teaching, a teaching style encouraging student engagement by providing opportunities to grapple with and discover knowledge. Activities should include manipulating, classifying, and creating. Conceptual development teaching increases motivation by allowing students to take ownership of their learning. Students have the opportunity to explore concepts and acquire their own knowledge and understanding. Direct instruction may be beneficial to use after conceptual development activities as teachers scaffold and make sure students are progressing appropriately.

Another option for teachers is inquiry-based learning. Inquiry-based teaching increases students' motivation to learn. This style creates an environment in which students actively participate in the learning process. It encourages them to take responsibility, set goals, and monitor their progress. Since inquiry-based learning covers multiple learning objectives, teachers can slow their pace and guide students through deep, relevant explorations instead of vaguely covering content. It also allows teachers to facilitate the lesson while students communicate, think critically, and explain their knowledge to others.

The flipped classroom was mentioned earlier. When teachers flip their classrooms, they change the order of how and when information is presented. This strategy can take many forms. Usually, the teacher gives students an assignment to complete at home to build curiosity. The assignment can be recorded lessons with the presentation of a challenge or mystery, digital presentation media, virtual manipulative, or educational videos. The next day in person, students can share thoughts, and the teacher can go deeper into the content. The end of the lesson can consist of inquiry-based activities. In this section's opening, I described how I use the flipped classroom model to prepare teacher candidates. This teaching strategy is excellent for those who enjoy mixing up teaching styles.

The Importance of Innovation and Problem-Solving

When used appropriately, all four of these teaching styles allow students to be innovative problem-solvers. COVID-19 thrust us into an unknown environment forcing us to make adjustments. These transitions challenged us all. We courageously accepted this endeavor because we knew our children would be scared if we were scared. We became the problem-solvers for this generation. Our children and grandchildren will become the problem-solvers of their generation. We are and will have to continue being innovative as we come up with solutions. Innovative does not mean being a guru in a particular field of study. Instead, it means being able to brainstorm solutions and enact one of those solutions to solve a problem. Our families are being innovative every day by finding solutions to societal problems as a result of COVID-19. For example, people are designing unique masks to protect us from airborne particles, and we are also seeing transparent shower curtains being used to help individuals safely hug their loved ones. Innovative thinking happens when multiple forces join together for a common cause. Innovation through the years cannot be attributed to one individual. Similarly, education started with more than one educator formulating solutions to our problems. Therefore, education should be revamped continually to formulate additional innovative solutions to new circumstances.

Think about the important historical contributions we have heard. There were problems to be solved, so individuals worked together to make changes efficiently. Going back to the 1800s and early 1900s, Henry Ford and Thomas Edison, along with many others, brainstormed answers for their generation's problems. The world had concerns, and these individuals worked extensively to address them. Cars and light bulbs were answers to some of their problems. These innovators brainstormed multiple solutions and experimented with each one to see if any worked. These projects were not completed in isolation. I am sure these inventors had multiple sounding boards as they tossed ideas back and forth among the group. Today, ideas and solutions still need to be tossed around as we travel down the path to our children's future. If we spend time showing students how to be innovative, they will be problem-solvers who make positive contributions to society. The ability to brainstorm and generate ideas are cultivated in safe and open learning environments.

Sometimes we make the mistake of trying to motivate students by doing what we believe intrigues them. For example, singing and dancing are not my talents. However, these may be the talents of my students. I should not have to force myself to sing and dance to engage and motivate my students. All I have to do is give them opportunities to use their talents, which may be singing and dancing. This engages them and increases their motivation as they begin to share their talents and feel a sense of belonging. To continue promoting a growth-mindset, students should know their opinion matters. Do not be afraid to ask them what they think about hybrid learning and what changes they suggest. When active in the learning process, students will not think they have to sit passively as knowledge is gradually released. Engagement is more than students listening passively to pass a class. Our objective is to encourage students to discover knowledge on their own. When we present information in an engaging way, students will listen as they search for the answers needed to proceed forward in their interactive assignments. The right teaching style at the right time can spark curiosity and creativity.

Consider this scenario: one Friday after work, a coworker is kidnapped. I know, I cannot believe it happened on a Friday either. Her kidnappers led her to a building with three doors, each leading to three separate rooms. They told her she could pick whichever door she wanted; however, they warned her to pick wisely. Behind door number one are sumo wrestlers ready to brawl. Behind door number two are lions who have not eaten in years. Behind door number three is a blazing fire. Which door should she pick?

Above is another example of an attention-grabbing lateral thinking activity. We can help students think creatively by embracing curiosity and opening students' minds as they become comfortable sharing their ideas. In the above scenario, hopefully, door number two was selected because the lions are dead. Several teaching styles can be used to boost curiosity and engagement. Teachers do not have to pick one teaching style and stick with it all year. Multiple styles can be intertwined to accomplish content goals.

Carefully selecting teaching styles is vital when creating lessons for hybrid learning environments. With whole group instruction, it is hard to see which students are hiding behind other students. Sometimes struggling learners wait for the perceived "smart" student to answer the question. Teaching styles should permit students to strengthen their critical, creative, and problem-solving thinking skills. By varying teaching styles, teachers can facilitate learning and monitor progress to ensure all students are comprehending and understanding. In addition to effective teaching styles, there are growth cycles educators should consider when planning lessons.

NOTES

CHAPTER 3
APPLYING EDUCATIONAL THEORIES
Growth Cycles in Maslow's, Piaget's, and Bloom's Educational Models

"What is necessary to change a person is to change his awareness of himself."
~Abraham Maslow

"If you want to be creative, stay in part a child, with the creativity and invention that characterizes children before they are deformed by adult society."
~ Jean Piaget

"What any person in the world can learn, almost all persons can learn if provided with appropriate and current pathways to learning."
~Benjamin Bloom

What do water, the butterfly, and the plant cycles have in common? They all allow us to make predictions because they are continuously looping, allowing viewers to infer what stage is coming next. We will examine a new way to look at Abraham Maslow's, Jean Piaget's, and Benjamin Bloom's development models and each one's relevancy. Educators studied these theories in college; however, we did not have opportunities to apply our new knowledge. As with the water cycle, the educational models we will discuss should be seen as a circular loop constantly cycling between each level. Both children and adults continuously travel through these levels daily. This chapter will explain the circular patterns found in these models and provide practical strategies and teaching styles to create effective hybrid learning lessons.

Abraham Maslow's Hierarchy of Needs

Maslow's Hierarchy of Needs can increase the effectiveness of classroom management strategies by accounting for each level's needs. This model's base level covers students' needs for air, food, water, and shelter. Once this need is met, students assess their environment to make sure they are safe and secure. Love and belonging are achieved when students are free to express themselves. The last level, referred to as self-actualization, is fulfilled as students brainstorm, share, and create. Students begin to trust others, which builds self-confidence and encourages them to share their talents. Maslow's hierarchy model is displayed vertically, which leads some people to believe it ends or tops out. When presented vertically or as a pyramid, it appears to follow the progression of an elevator: the higher the level, the closer the individual is to reaching the top. Abraham Maslow did not intend for his model to be seen in a gaming format in which players level up after completing the previous level. This model was created to explain the levels; however, Maslow's intentions are better understood when the model is displayed as a circular cycle. Interestingly, many people fail to realize that Maslow's Hierarchy of Needs also describes the needs of adults.

Let's look at an example showing how Maslow's Hierarchy of Needs applies to adults. Think about the last time you started a new job. You were probably nervous and worried because you did not know anyone. You secretly hoped someone would reach out and take you under their wing. You needed a work friend. Once found, I bet he or she helped you build your confidence and surpass your work expectations. The third level of Maslow's Hierarchy of Needs, the need to feel love and belonging, had been met, and you knew you belonged with your company.

When we talk about the importance of Maslow's Hierarchy of Needs, our focus should be on creating the right environment to optimize learning. Maslow's Hierarchy of Needs shows the conditions needed to motivate individuals intrinsically. Notice it specifies individuals, as opposed to only children. This means that, as adults, we are constantly seeking ways to fulfill our needs. Need another example of not having your needs met? Have you ever been *hangry*?

The educational theories we will discuss were designed to be fluid and not a fixed order of levels to be mastered. Maslow's Hierarchy of Needs should be seen as a continuous cycle. The model displayed below shows the stages we may be going through at any given point in time.

Figure 1: Hierarchy of Needs viewed as a circular pattern

We are our best selves when we are at the self-actualization level. As educators, we must be aware of this cycle so we can constantly assess our students' needs. Fulfilling these needs enables students to open their minds to learning. The next page will show examples of how students may behave at each stage and appropriate responses to properly support them.

BASIC NEEDS: Being provided daily with air, food, water, shelter, and sleep

Adverse behaviors 1: being hungry, *hangry*, or thirsty

Responses: provide snacks, allow them to bring a snack or water bottle, encourage them to eat at lunch

Adverse behaviors 2: constantly sleeping

Responses: show understanding, ask questions such as, "Would it help if you stood up to do your work?" "Do you want to talk about it?" and "Is there anything I can do to help?"

SAFETY AND SECURITY: Feeling secure in an environment, having all social and emotional needs met, and living a healthy lifestyle

Adverse behaviors: small amount of talking and sharing, scared to work in groups, afraid to take responsibility for behavior and work, flinching or continuously looking over their shoulders

Responses: consistently encourage students to ask questions, let them know asking questions also helps their classmates, and post agendas to guide students

LOVE AND BELONGING: Feeling a sense of belonging in a group and able to express feelings and thoughts

Adverse behaviors: attention-seeking, hanging out with negative influences, not liking school or teachers

Responses: ask other teachers to be a mentor, help them feel a sense of belonging by asking them to share their thoughts, opportunities to show their talents, place them around friendly peers, show care and concern both verbally and nonverbally

ESTEEM: Having high levels of self-esteem, feeling confident, feeling respected and valued by others, and having a sense of purpose

Adverse behaviors: being needy, feeling sad while at school, not motivated, displaying shyness, not interacting with peers in class or outside of class

Responses: incorporate more collaboration, provide opportunities for students to focus on their strengths, offer words of encouragement, and utilize strategies for classmates to encourage one another

SELF-ACTUALIZATION: Being intrinsically motivated and feeling free to take risks and be creative

Adverse behaviors: expressing feeling worthless, not participating, depending on the ideas of others, unmotivated

Responses: allow students to solve problems their way as long as they can prove the answer is correct, provide active opportunities for the student to experiment with multiple career options, encourage them to follow their dreams

Students and adults travel this loop daily. As educators, we should be understanding of our students' situations and offer support when needed. Let's discuss some of the Dos and Don'ts of meeting our students' needs.

Table 1	BASIC NEEDS
DO	**DO NOT**
Be understanding	Make excuses
Provide items needed (if possible)	Ignore their needs

Table 2	SAFE and SECURE
DO	**DO NOT**
Set high expectations	Lower standards because of their situation
Establish rules and procedures	Allow chaos and ignore misbehavior
Create a safe environment	Allow bullying, teasing, or "just kidding" behaviors

Table 3	LOVE and BELONGING

DO	DO NOT
Be understanding	Make excuses
Maintain high expectations for all	Lower expectations in an attempt to sympathize with them
Talk positively and have a positive attitude (positive check-ins such as a fist bump or quick chats upon entering the class environment)	Talk negatively or allow others to talk negatively or shame others
Respect students (Respect is an abstract concept. Be sure to discuss with students about how respect looks, sounds, and feels)	Expect them to come to class knowing what respect means (regardless of their age)
Build relationships (share stories and interact with them)	Pretend or stay in "serious" mode in order for them to comply

Table 4	ESTEEM

DO	DO NOT
Be understanding	Make excuses
Build students' intrinsic motivation	Give too many external rewards as an effort to increase their motivation
Give students relevant assignments and tasks	Provide assignments that are not challenging, giving students a false perception of their skills and talents
Provide opportunities for students to share their input	Always provide the answer before they have time to reflect
Focus on students' strengths and recognize their potential	Obsess over their weaknesses (Students know the weaknesses are there but may be too embarrassed to give it their best effort when teachers only focus on the weaknesses day after day)
Love is an action verb, so do not be afraid to show it. Remember: We *win from within*	Just say "I love you."

16

Table 5	SELF-ACTUALIZATION	

DO	DO NOT
Give students hope and a vision of success	Hinder their dreams by telling them what they cannot do or be
Show students where to look but not what to see	Limit their possibilities by leading them down one pathway
Promote growth mindsets and self-reflection as students analyze their mistakes in a safe environment	Shame or punish them for giving the wrong answer or making a mistake
Help students see their purpose and talents	Focus only on areas of weakness

Maslow's Hierarchy of Needs is one of the theories we will apply to make hybrid learning lessons. Hopefully this new view of our students' needs clarified misconceptions and provided suitable suggestions for a hybrid learning class environment. In the next session, Jean Piaget's Theory of Cognitive Development will be analyzed.

NOTES

Jean Piaget's Theory of Cognitive Development

Jean Piaget is the psychologist who developed the theory of cognitive development in 1936. The purpose of his research was to explain the development of children at different ages. Remember, all new learning objectives are abstract to students. We may think an assignment is age-appropriate, but it may be difficult to understand based on the depth level of the assignment. The stages of cognitive development are sensorimotor, preoperational, concrete, and formal operational. While reading the descriptions below, notice the suggested age range for each stage.

- Sensorimotor- knowing an object exists (birth to 18-24 months)

- Preoperational- discovering learning by playing with objects (toddler to approximately age 7)

- Concrete operational- using manipulatives to explore knowledge and concepts (ages 7 to 11)

- Formal operational- using abstract thinking, which is the ability to learn and show knowledge and concepts without manipulatives (adolescent to adulthood- ages 12 and up)

In Piaget's theory, the average age range is given; however, the ages and learning rates are not fixed. As with Maslow's Hierarchy of Needs, students continuously progress through these stages as they learn new concepts.

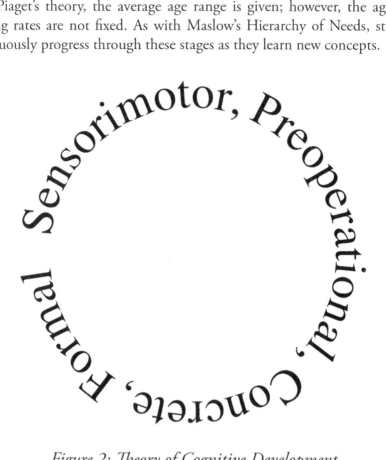

Figure 2: Theory of Cognitive Development

We should not expect students to enter our class environment with the same level of knowledge as adults. When I first began teaching fourth grade, I made the mistake of going straight to the formal operational stage because it was how I learned. I remember thinking of songs and mnemonics to help my students recall information. I even tried using shortcuts, such as the butterfly method for comparing and multiplying fractions. In English Language Arts, I tried teaching my students how to use their fingers to name and identify text structures. However, these methods failed to show my students what we were doing and why we were doing it. To be honest, these ineffective strategies probably made my students more confused. I had to learn to develop my students' knowledge by teaching at their current cognitive development level. When I moved to the middle school setting, I noticed my students still needed concrete manipulatives even though they were older, which helped me understand the importance of allowing students to grapple with and explore content. Standing at the board, teaching steps to solve problems, and reviewing content definitions were not beneficial. I started searching for manipulatives. For example, I bought 3D shapes to teach volume and surface area. My students also brought real-world examples of 3D shapes to class, such as cereal boxes and canned foods. When I taught positive and negative numbers, I took a problem set found in our math resources, printed the activity on cardstock, and cut the pieces so students could sort them based on realworld situations. For instance, a card saying "scored two points in basketball" would go in the positive column, and a card saying "below sea level" would go in the negative column. These methods can also be used in other subjects to provide tangible and concrete materials as students learn concepts.

Another example of how I guided my students through the stages of cognitive development occurred after I received a class set of iPads. Online learning tools allowed my students to virtually explore and manipulate items. Online learning tools were beneficial because I did not always have manipulatives on hand. The iPads also enabled students to use everyday resources, such as nutritional and workout apps, to analyze and apply knowledge. Scaffolding through the cognitive development stages gradually moved my students from concrete to abstract thinking. Educators know that students' knowledge is commonly assessed at stage four on standardized assessments, asking them to justify their answers. Using Piaget's Theory of Cognitive Development, educators can visually show students what they are doing before teaching them how to complete problems without aides.

Benjamin Bloom's Taxonomy of Cognitive Skills

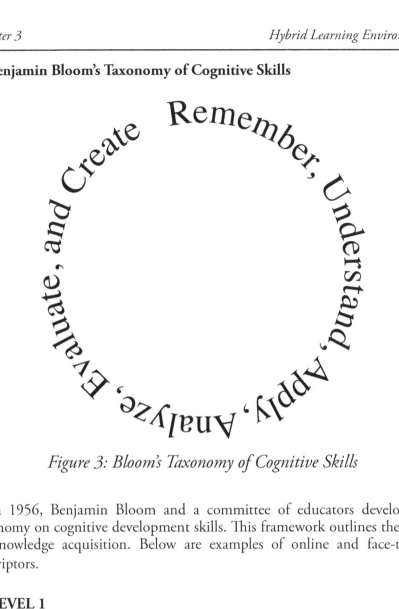

Figure 3: Bloom's Taxonomy of Cognitive Skills

In 1956, Benjamin Bloom and a committee of educators developed a taxonomy on cognitive development skills. This framework outlines the level of knowledge acquisition. Below are examples of online and face-to-face descriptors.

LEVEL 1
The Remember level involves defining terms, identifying facts, and reviewing information.

- Face-to-face: direct instruction from the teacher, students search for examples in their environment, and work independently or with a partner to review and practice

- Online: video clips, vivid examples from around the world, and complete interactive review and practice games

LEVEL 1

The Understand level provides opportunities for students to explain ideas or concepts. This level moves students from recognizing information to understanding and involves retelling, providing their own examples, summarizing, and inferring.

- Face-to-face: concept development using hands-on in classroom activities with a partner

- Online: concept development using online manipulatives, virtual partner or small group

LEVEL 2

The Apply level allows students to demonstrate their knowledge and apply content. On this level, students can manipulate, demonstrate, discover, and illustrate.

- Face-to-face: scaffolding from concrete to abstract, students visually show their understanding and comprehension. Activities can include collages, posters, or brochures showing real-world understanding.

- Online: scaffolding from concrete to abstract, students visually show their understanding and comprehension. Activities may include virtual collages, posters, or brochures showing real-world understanding.

LEVEL 3

The Analyze level allows students to analyze, compare, determine relationships, and sync new knowledge with background knowledge. Students should have time to reflect, deconstruct, and integrate knowledge.

- Face-to-face: probing questions, productive struggle, using the scientific method, and debates

- Online: probing questions, productive struggle, using the scientific method, and debates

LEVEL 4

The Evaluating level lets students reason, justify, and monitor their content knowledge.

- Face-to-face: opportunities to explain reasoning, use rubrics and checklists, and gain feedback from teacher and peers

- Online: opportunities to virtually explain reasoning, use rubrics and checklists, and gain feedback from teacher and peers

LEVEL 4

At the Create level, students brainstorm ideas, devise a plan, produce solutions, and present materials or final projects to others.

- Face-to-face: student-led activities, inquiry-based, and creation of projects and products
- Online: student-led activities, inquiry-based, technology-enhanced creation of projects and products

When seen as a circular cycle, Bloom's Taxonomy levels enable instructors to scaffold lessons and provide opportunities to cycle through each level based on individual, small group, and whole group struggling needs. To increase students' intrinsic motivation, consider starting each lesson with hands-on activities, explorations, and manipulatives. The last two chapters of this book will discuss integrating teaching styles and applying the three growth cycles in hybrid learning environments and lesson planning.

NOTES

CHAPTER 4
OPTIMAL LEARNING ENVIRONMENTS

"Logic will get you from A to B. Imagination will take you EVERYWHERE."
~ Albert Einstein

"How can I ever increase my test scores if my students will not listen? I give them directions, but they still interrupt me to ask questions I have already answered." Does this sound familiar? I was in the same predicament. By asking the right question at the right time, I was able to create the right class environment to resolve this question. I asked my curriculum specialist what I could do to actively involve my students. Her response was, "Stop putting your desks in rows because you are subconsciously telling them to only listen." She went on to say, "Sitting quietly and listening does not mean your students are acquiring knowledge." I knew I had to get comfortable with my students working in pairs. After trying it out a few times, I noticed my students enjoyed the new setup and wanted more engagement. Initially, I thought my students would play around with their friends, and I would see an increase in behavior problems. However, I soon realized there is a difference between talk and *productive* talk, and I was able to see active engagement instead of passive listening. I started focusing on keeping them engaged because I needed my students to stay motivated. Students are safe to collaborate, share, and trust in optimal learning environments because they have a sense of belonging.

Trying to determine the underlying issue of a student's behavior is a challenge. It could be a lack of motivation or a bad situation at home causing them to seek attention. We can spend all day trying to figure out the issue, but even if we did, what could we do about it? Focusing on active engagement and motivation creates an environment where students can leave their problems at home. Optimal hybrid learning environments allow students to stay motivated as they find their value. Students learn to value others when they value themselves. Whether online or in-person, students deserve to be in the right class environment. Using classroom management strategies for an optimal in-person class and establishing etiquettes for an optimal online class creates a compelling hybrid learning environment. Remember, the phrase "hybrid" refers to learning that can be taught in any environment. In this chapter, we will examine how to create optimal learning environments for online and in-person classes.

An optimal learning environment must be structured while also igniting curiosity and intrinsic motivation. Students respond to their surroundings. If the class environment is chaotic, students will behave chaotically. If loud talking is permitted in one group, all groups will feel the need to talk louder in order to project their voice to group members. Consequently, not having clear boundaries can hinder students' thinking. Active engagement should be centered around students' needs. Once these needs are met, students will be able to learn in a risk-free environment. To set boundaries, students need to know what they can and cannot do. At the beginning of the school year, teachers may need to use online and face-to-face role-play to show students how to behave appropriately and offer feedback without bickering or being mean. Expectations should be modeled and reviewed frequently. Children are less likely to forget the expectations if the rules and procedures are reviewed every two or three weeks. I once believed that explaining the rules for the first two weeks of school would be sufficient enough to attain effective classroom management. However, I realized students do not forget the rules; instead they patiently wait for teachers to forget them. Consistently reviewing rules and procedures will ensure students understand appropriate behavior expectations throughout the school year. For example, if I am doing a hands-on lesson, I need to explain to my students why they should not do something and the consequences of their actions. Children are naturally curious, so whenever we say, "do not," we need to follow up with the reason behind this phrase. Always replace what students cannot do with what they can do. Active engagement cannot happen in an unstructured environment. The chart on the next page shows what active engagement is and what it is not.

Table 6	ACTIVE ENGAGEMENT	
IS		**IS NOT**
having educational discussions with group members		laughing, joking, or playing around
listening for details necessary to complete a task		passively listening
having fun by exploring, creating, and experimenting		having fun while playing
educational talk with the ability to quiet down		Off-topic talking with a lack of respect

Let's go deeper and discuss what an optimal learning environment looks, feels, and sounds like. Optimal learning environments look like busy ants working together to achieve a goal. Teachers are facilitators moving around the room, or in and out of chat meeting rooms, to guide students' learning. Students can lean on their peers and move to other portions of their task as they wait for their teacher to come to their group or enter their chat room. Checking on each group frequently allows teachers to ask questions and check for understanding. In optimal learning environments, teachers should also see students collaborating with peers, taking responsibility for their learning, and becoming more self-sufficient.

What do optimal learning environments feel like? Optimal learning environments feel like you are free to exhale and be yourself. As students enter the learning environment, they should know they can be themselves in class. They should feel comfortable relaxing and enjoying the moment, whether at home or in class, because they know they are loved. They should also feel safe knowing no one will harm them physically, mentally, or emotionally. Students should know their classmates are not going to laugh at their thoughts and ideas. They should not fear embarrassment, and they should feel comfortable asking questions and receiving feedback. In this environment, students safely take risks and explore. Instructors can begin creating this environment by allowing students to share their viewpoints. At the beginning of the school year, ask students to share something about themselves to help classmates get to know them better. I suggest doing this throughout the school year so the class can continue growing close with each other. For example, the teacher may post, "What animal best describes your personality and why?" or "Upload a picture of your favorite activity." Quick engagement opportunities such as these help students feel valued as they share with peers.

What do optimal learning environments sound like? Optimal learning environments sound like small gadgets working together in sync. As facilitation takes place, one should hear collaboration and communication as students toss around ideas. This talk should be positive and productive as students are mindful of how they treat their peers. Administrators and parents might walk by to see what all the noise is about, only to find themselves wanting to stop and join in on the fun. Productive noise from collaboration and communication is a sign of active engagement. Teachers should embrace these moments and create them as often as possible. Optimal hybrid learning environments naturally motivate students because they are free to explore, collaborate, and innovate.

P.S.- the "What does it look like, feel like, and sound like" template is an excellent model to use when explaining abstract concepts, such as being respectful.

Lastly, an optimal learning environment includes effective communication with students and parents. Whether in-person or online, the goal is to make personal connections with students. Students need our love and support. Sometimes our greetings are the first words of encouragement they have heard all day. Teacher and student online communication can be conducted via discussion boards, marker boards, and interactive chats. Teachers can connect with students by asking sincere questions: How are you feeling today? What are you looking forward to? and What picture or color would you select to tell how you are feeling? Remember, students who show feelings and emotions the least need the connections the most. Therefore, there can never be too much interaction. Additionally, not having enough interaction can cause students to feel the teacher only cares about their work. We know our students need personal connections and love. Be sure to be creative as you show yours.

When communicating with parents, the main concern they will have is if their child is safe. An unsafe environment encompasses more than physical harm. Safe and secure also means knowing students are not socially or emotionally hurt by strangers or peers when face-to-face and online. It means all students feel included and valued. Being proactive about students' social and emotional needs helps parents relax and trust their child's teacher. To partner with parents for the betterment of their child, be considerate of their jobs and actively open the lines of communication in the beginning. They will appreciate it. Parents will have many questions about work tasks. We can help our parents help us by making sure they know exactly what is going on in class. Keep parents and students in the loop by providing a user-friendly agenda each day. It should be posted and shared in multiple locations. One of the best ways to help parents feel comfortable is by providing timely information and being understanding when discussing concerns and solutions. Optimal learning environments produce collaboration, in-depth thinking, and positive social and emotional interactions. Optimal learning cannot take place in isolation. Optimal hybrid learning environments are created by working to fulfill adults' and students' needs. The right class environment supports students, parents, and teachers as students discover their strengths and talents. The last chapter of this book will focus on how to combine the information acquired so far and use it to create effective hybrid learning lesson plans.

CHAPTER 5
EASY PEASY LESSON PLANS

"Education is the kindling of a flame not the filling of a vessel."
~ Socrates

This chapter will present strategies and lesson plans to promote growth mindsets, active engagement, and intrinsic motivation. These activities empower students to discover their own knowledge and skills with teacher support. Teaching styles, applicable educational theories, and optimal classroom environments will be integrated to plan and create effective hybrid learning lessons. Lesson plans should be created with proactive mindsets focused on how students will use the knowledge when they graduate and begin their careers. To be effective in-person and online, lesson plans should start with an activator, have active engagement in the middle, and close with a project or task to share knowledge with others. Remember, closure projects should not take longer than a week or week and a half to complete because students should be working on pieces of it throughout the week. Closing projects are not thematic units or problem-based tasks. Teachers mistakenly see it as a unit and lose many hours of instruction trying to give students time to complete long-term projects. Closing projects can be completed when students have extra time, during center times, or in small groups. Here is an example of useful lesson plan components:

1. Activator to wake up the brain: provide thought-provoking challenge, mystery, or Science, Technology, Engineering, and Mathematics (STEM) activity.

2. Opportunity to share: host a quick discussion for thoughts and feelings.

3. Middle engagement: have students build their own knowledge by exploring, manipulating, or sorting important information. ELA example:

use premade informational sheets with three examples showing reputable information and three examples showing non-reputable information to research and cite evidence for students to sort into piles. Math example use pre-cut pictures showing what fractions are and what they are not for students to sort to help students understand fractional parts.

4. End- Let students analyze and apply. For instance, create a picture showing an example of what the topic is and another example showing what it is not. Using art activities allow students to critically think as they find ways to express their knowledge.

5. Progress- Monitor progress and check for understanding with exit cards, a question survey, discussions, 3-5 problems asked the right way (explained later), or a formal assessment.

6. Closure- Share understanding in a new and creative way by allowing students to show what they have learned. This can be done by using the content in real-world scenarios and asking students to complete a task. For example, in ELA, students can write a memo to a CEO (classmate) using two different text structures to explain if landline phones should be eliminated. In math, students can create a digital collage showing fractions in the real-world. The collage can be pictures of medical tools, measuring cups, football fields, time, gas tanks, and other related items.

The sample lesson steps above show active student engagement, which is how hybrid learning lessons should start and end. A hybrid lesson plan contains effective steps from both online and in-person lessons. Both the virtual lesson and the face-to-face lesson steps should be formatted to accomplish the same goal. The teacher will then be able to choose any step from either lesson plan to create a hybrid learning lesson. Essentially, the best face-to-face lesson steps and the best online lesson steps can be selected from either source to make the best hybrid learning lesson. Here is one example of how the steps may appear in a four-step lesson plan. Step one: an activity from an online lesson plan; step two: an activity from a face-to-face lesson plan; step three: a face-to-face lesson plan activity; and step four: an online lesson plan activity. The activities can be arranged in any order because the order does not change the effectiveness.

As educators, it is easy to begin a lesson believing our students have the necessary background knowledge. However, we should consider every lesson content as an abstract concept for students. Even something as "simple" as adding numbers is an abstract concept when students start learning it, which explains the importance of scaffolding and applying the theories discussed earlier. To start the lesson off smoothly, post a student-friendly agenda each day. A blueprint for a house guides the builder's steps. Agendas do the same thing: provide the steps without completing the task. An engaging lesson should have at least one engaging task at the beginning, middle, and end. The following sections will show how teaching may look during each section of learning. When planning engaging lessons, consider these questions:

- Why do students need to know this?
- When are they ever going to use this in life?
- Where do we see this concept in real life?
- What do I need students to know by the end of this concept lesson?
- How will I guide students to complete understanding and utilization of this concept?

These questions promote proactive thinking while developing a lesson. They also provide clues as to what the teacher should look for when inspecting learning. Below are two examples of completed lesson plans for face-to-face and online learning.

Lesson Plan #1
Math-Understanding Fractions, Decimals, and Percent

By Melanie Wells

Essential Question: How many different ways can you represent an amount?

Objectives:

1. Understand a fraction $1/b$ as the quantity formed by 1 part when a whole is partitioned into b equal parts.

2. Understand a fraction as a number on the number line; represent fractions on a number line diagram.

3. Represent a fraction $1/b$ on a number line diagram by defining the interval from 0 to 1 as the whole and partitioning it into b equal parts.

Learning Targets:

• I can represent an amount in various ways.

• I can demonstrate my understanding of fractions, decimals, and percent using a picture and number line.

Conceptual Understanding:

1. An amount can be represented as a fraction, decimal, and percent.

2. This equivalency can be visualized using a picture and number line.

3. The denominator shows how many parts the number line should be divided into, and the numerator indicates how many meet the criteria.

Lesson Steps:

1. Introduction: Ask, "What are fractions?" Listen to all responses, but do not correct or assist students with their answers.

2. Explore: Working with a partner, students will complete a sorting activity on fractions. Post or print picture cards showing what fractions are and what they are not. This activity is designed to clarify common misconceptions about fractions.

3. Discussion: Discuss any misconceptions with students.

4. Essential Question: How many different ways can an amount be represented?

5. Activity: Display fractions found online on the board and ask students how many different ways can that amount be represented. Working in pairs, students will complete an activity on matching a fraction with its appropriate picture and number line.

6. Activity (visual representation): Students should understand that a fraction is part of a whole OR part of a set. Allow students to view real-world pictures of fractional parts. Model how to represent each one on a labeled number line showing the amount as a fraction, decimal, and percent. Allow students to use a tangible or online whiteboard to display their results individually. Teach students how to divide a number line based on the total number of parts (the denominator). As students fill in their own number lines, they should also begin to understand that the fraction bar means to divide and shows how many times to split the amount. Pictures such as an online ruler, soda pops, starbursts, and many others can be enlarged to help students understand.

7. Check for understanding: give students an exit card slip with three fractions and ask students to create a number line labeled with the correct fraction, decimal, and percent.

Lesson Plan #2
ELA- Analyzing Texts and Poems

By Melanie Wells

Essential Question: How do you know you are following along with the book you are reading?

Objectives:

1. RL Standard 1: Cite textual evidence to support analysis of what the text says explicitly as well as inferences drawn from the text.

2. RL Standard 2: Determine a theme of a story, drama, or poem from details in the text, including how characters in a story or drama respond to challenges or how the speaker in a poem reflects upon a topic; summarize the text.

3. RL Standard 4: Determine the meaning of words and phrases as they are used in the text, including figurative and connotative meanings.

4. RL Standard 5: Explain how a series of chapters, scenes, or stanzas fits together to provide the overall structure of a particular story, drama, or poem.

Learning Targets:

• I can cite evidence from literary text to support my analysis.

• I can determine a theme based on details in the text.

• I can determine the meaning of literal and figurative language (metaphors and similes) in text.

• I can analyze how a particular sentence, stanza, scene, or chapter fits in and contributes to the development of a text.

Conceptual Understanding:

One way to help students comprehend as they are reading is to stop often and ask students to explain the story playing in their head. When reading for understanding, there should be a visual image or movie playing as students are reading paragraph by paragraph.

Lesson Steps:

1. Activator (hook)- Show a short movie trailer on a relevant and appropriate movie.

2. Model and discuss- Spend time modeling metacognition with students. Allow students to share different views they may have in their minds.

3. Essential Question: What movie is playing in your head?

4. Activity: Poems can be a challenge for students. Here is a suggested activity: break students into groups of 3-5. Have each student create and label a picture depicting a stanza of a pre-selected poem (students need to label the items in the picture to make sure they thoroughly analyzed it). After students have drawn their stanza, tell them to form groups based on their stanzas. For example, all students with stanza one will meet and discuss what they drew and why (the teacher may need to post the discussion questions). After students return to their original group, they take turns explaining the picture they created for their stanza to complete the whole poem. Lastly, students will place their stanzas and pictures together, take a picture, and display their work digitally on a display screen to explain it to the class.

5. Check for understanding: Teacher facilitation and prompting questions to allow students to explain their thinking.

6. Discussion: Closure and discussion on the purpose of the task and relating them to different types of documents. Allow students to practice visualizing story elements by providing various documents throughout the year for students to discuss the movie they see playing in their heads.

After viewing these two lesson plans, it is important to notice they do not show days. This is because lesson plans may vary from day to day depending on how students need to be scaffolded. On the other hand, notice the detailed lesson steps. Even if a teacher has to slow down, she or he will already know the level of complexity necessary to master the content. Being proactive and detailed at the beginning keeps the teacher on track and ensures deep conceptual understanding.

As a mentor for first-year teachers, I experienced first-hand how intentional and meticulous one must be when trying to conduct a lesson. After observing my class, a new teacher commented on my "with-it-ness," a term meaning to flow smoothly as if it was pre-orchestrated. What is interesting is that she knew the phrase but could not apply the concept of "with-it-ness" in her class. I wondered why she did not know how to apply the phrase in her lesson so it would flow smoothly. I soon realized she struggled with anticipating students' behaviors and misconceptions. I spent time reflecting on how to teach someone how to teach. I was reminded of a time when I was teaching my younger sister to drive. Driving, like teaching, is usually done almost effortlessly once mastered. Still, knowing how to drive was an abstract concept for my sister in the beginning. To teach her this skill, I broke down each step to explain what to do and how it would feel. I used relatable examples to guide her knowledge. For instance, I told her acceleration was similar to drinking hot coffee. Coffee drinkers know what to expect and slowly tip their cup to avoid burning their tongue. Using this same concept, I was able to explain how the accelerator and brake pedals work. When accelerating and braking, one should slowly ease off the pedal because they will not have a smooth transition if they do not. I use this same step-by-step approach to show new teachers how to be effective. My mentee and I would spend time role-playing different scenarios and lessons. I would ask thought-provoking questions to help her reflect on the lesson. I would also assume the role of a misbehaving child so she could practice how to respond. My goal for her was the same as my goal for my readers: break down and scaffold lessons into understandable pieces that fit together to complete a puzzle.

Why Not Just Use my Textbook?

It is hard to find a lesson in a textbook that will encompass high levels of learning. Therefore, teachers may need to spend time thinking outside the confines of a traditional textbook. For example, when I wanted my students to understand and apply knowledge on charts and graphs, I had to explore real-world options. I used a cell phone and apps like "Nike Run" and "Calorie Counter" to create tasks involving everyday situations. Because a textbook wants the reader to master the lesson and keep buying their products, the lessons have lesson steps on a "low to medium" level. The text is designed for the average student. Sometimes the textbook includes enrichment and remediation suggestions, but they do not teach comprehension or application. Textbooks should be used as a resource, not as a curriculum. When creating lessons, think about the products we engage with daily. This thought process results in outside-the-box thinking and relatable teaching.

Many times, we feel we need to lower the content level for our struggling students. We believe starting with a challenging activity when we have not covered the basics will leave students confused. However, it is beneficial for students to develop their own understanding through exposure because it piques their curiosity. Consider deep-sea diving. Even if students must start with their toes in the water, they still receive the full experience because the lifeguard or scuba instructor is their safety net. We cannot prepare students to swim by telling them how to swim. They must jump in the water and complete the steps on their own with our encouragement and guidance. Moving this scenario back to the class environment, students will not mind listening to the instructor as she or he guides them because they know they are gaining vital information needed to learn the concept. Our goal is to allow students to explore and develop their own knowledge to accomplish the task.

How Can I Help my Students be Engaged all the Time?

Think about the best lesson you have taught. I am talking about the lesson where you had the most *Aha Moments*. Think about that day for a few minutes. What was different about this particular lesson? What happened in this lesson that rarely happens in others? More importantly, how can you engage students like this all the time? During your best lesson, you probably noticed students asking tons of questions. Their curiosity was running wild. They anticipated what would happen next. And, I can see them talking and collaborating, probably on the edge of their seats having productive educational talk. Take a moment to reflect on what you did differently. The next sections will provide strategies and examples for creating this type of lesson over and over again. Details on how to effectively build curiosity and engagement by implementing effective teaching styles and scaffolding lessons will also be provided.

Effectively Merge Teaching Styles

There are several teaching styles utilized in in-person and online classes. As a new teacher, I made the mistake of focusing on one. My students would have accomplished more if I had spent time merging my teaching styles based on how I needed to scaffold my students through the lesson. When I started my educational career teaching fourth grade, I remember watching one of my students struggle in my classroom. He did not understand concepts in whole group, small group, or one-on-one instruction. It struggled with how to help him because I could not determine where he needed help. One day, I searched through the previous teacher's materials and found several money manipulative packs. Money was the topic I was currently teaching, so I decided to try a hands-on lesson. To be honest, I had no idea how the lesson would turn out. I did not know if my students would have good behavior as they engaged with the manipulatives. I pulled out the money trays and wrote different values on the board for them to count out. I noticed my student who had been struggling all year immediately caught on and was actively engaged in the activity. I looked at him after we worked a few more problems, and he was lying on the floor with his hands behind his head. He had a smile on his face as he waited for the next question. He was finally in his learning zone. What is interesting is that this student was in a fourth-grade class. It is tempting to think students should not need manipulatives past a certain grade. I could have easily said, "He should not need manipulatives because he has been learning to count money since second grade." This experience helped me understand the importance of meeting students where they are. The teaching styles we will merge are direct, conceptual, and inquiry-based instructions. Our intent should be to let students explore and find solutions without giving them the answer. Thankfully, they have us as their safety nets. We must be ready to jump in if we see them drowning. Consider the topic of quantum physics. If I was asked to explain quantum physics to someone, I would not be able to do it. I would need someone to scaffold a lesson on it. Providing a definition of quantum physics would not help me comprehend it. I need to know what it is, how it applies to the real world, and how to explain it to others. In addition, it would help if I saw concrete examples virtually or hands-on. After I have been given the opportunity to explore quantum physics, I can explain it to others. Even better, I might decide to pursue a career in quantum physics. Currently, I do not understand quantum physics, but I plan to do my research and explain it at the end of this book. Nevertheless, it is still an abstract concept. When we present content in an interesting way, students' curiosity will naturally grow, and they will want to dive into the content. A good starting point is building conceptual understanding.

Get Their Feet Wet by Building Conceptual Understanding

As we go through this planning process, notice how we skip Bloom's recalling and remembering levels. We will build their background knowledge by allowing them to explore the concept. Therefore, their background knowledge will be obtained by them and for them. Students can be engaged at the beginning of the day by activating their curiosity. Below is a list of online and face-to-face activators.

Table 7	LESSON ACTIVITIES- Conceptual Understanding	
Online:	**Opportunity to:**	**Face-to-Face:**
Record a media or audio-video clip and send it to a partner	**Discuss newly discovered knowledge**	Students discuss with a partner or make a human Likert scale to answer yes/no, true/false, agree/disagree questions
Insert text boxes in a word document or use an online sorting generator	**Make sense of info. Explore/sort/categorize**	Cut up premade informational pieces for students to sort
Relatable quotes, pictures, and optical illusions	**Reflect and analyze**	Relatable quotes, pictures, and optical illusions
Brainteaser, mystery story, guess my number, and others relatable to lesson topic	**Challenge**	Brainteaser, mystery story, guess my number, and others relatable to lesson topic
Concrete online manipulatives	**Hands-on exploration**	Concrete manipulatives online or in-person

Additional ideas can be found by searching keywords, such as science experiments, lateral thinking stories, divergent thinking, outside-the-box, activators, and real-world examples.

Dive Deeper to Explore and Deepen Knowledge

Once students' brains are open to learning, the teacher is ready to take them deeper into their thinking. Students are now prepared to swim in the content. The list below provides examples of activities at this level.

Table 8	LESSON ACTIVITIES- Deepening Knowledge	
Online:	**Opportunity to:**	**Face-to-Face:**
Whole group or small group (4-6 students) discussion using the	**Explain/Justify knowledge**	Whole group or small group (4-6 students) discussion in circular setups, such as Socratic method
communication platform of choice		
Group/Direct instruction (teacher can be visible online if desired)	**Clarify misconceptions**	Group/Direct instruction (teacher can be visible- online or face-to-face if desire)
Informational steps and directions (a map of what to do) visibly posted, printed, or displayed	**Prepare**	Informational steps and directions (a map of what to do) visibly posted, printed, or displayed

Create:
• a letter or memo
• a picture portraying the topic- for example, create a picture showing the relationship between positive and negative numbers
• a Venn Diagrams on difficult concepts like:
  1. the differences between two text structures
  2. how multiple authors build suspense in one book and how the same author builds suspense in another book
  3. whole numbers and fractions
  4. area and perimeter
	Actively engage Display knowledge in a personalized way	**Create:**
		• a letter or memo
		• a picture portraying the topic- for example, create a picture showing the relationship between positive and negative numbers
		• a Venn Diagrams on difficult concepts like:
		  1. the difference between two text structures
		  2. how multiple authors build suspense in one book and how the same author builds suspense in another book
		  3. whole numbers and fractions
		  4. area and perimeter

Assessments: exit cards, quick tasks, survey, informal and formal tests (can be completed both virtually and in-person)	**Check progress**	Assessments: exit cards, quick tasks, survey, informal and formal tests (can be completed both virtually and in-person)

A special note for designing quick assessment questions: think about what students needed to know for the particular lesson. For example, consider this order of operation problem with a common misconception embedded in it.

$$16 - 6 \div 2 \times 4 + 3 + 10$$

Instead of coming up with the correct answer of 17, misconceptions may produce 33 or 11. Remember, the right question asked the right way will help identify and correct misconceptions. This one problem assesses if students know how to follow the appropriate steps in the Order of Operations. One well-known mnemonic is PEMDAS (Parentheses, Exponents, Multiplication, Division, Addition, and Subtraction). In PEMDAS, multiplication and division, just like addition and subtraction, are completed in order from left to right as it appears in the problem. The PEMDAS mnemonic is an easy way to remember the operations; however, due to the way it is written, some students struggle to grasp the concept that each pair is on the same level. To correctly solve order of operation problems, work the problem in parentheses; the problems with exponents; the multiplication and division problems in the order they appear; and lastly, the addition and subtraction problems in the order they appear. This is one example of how asking the right question, the right way, will reveal students' misconceptions.

Deep-Sea Diving: Inquiry-Based Learning

The lesson is flowing, students are engaging, and content mastery is deepening. But wait, we are not finished. What if it is not a swimming pool? What if it is the ocean? Passion inspires, so let's go deep-sea diving!

Table 9	LESSON ACTIVITIES- Inquiry-Based Learning	
Online:	**Opportunity to:**	**Face-toFace:**
• Interactive websites • Online simulations • Completing group tasks virtually • Skype/Zoom around the world • Coding • Create digital collages or posters • Create a "Teachable Moments" video teaching the concept to peers • Create an educational game • Create a podcast or video • STEM tasks • Surveys- for example, "survey fifty people, use a graph maker to show results, complete a written or typed report on the findings, and present the information for others using a media platform, such as PowerPoint." (an excellent way to integrate multiple subjects)	• **Feel safe collaborating** • **Gain value and selfworth** • **Create and present** • **Show hidden and visual talents**	• Interactive websites • Online simulations • Completing group tasks face-to-face • Skype/Zoom around the world • Coding • Create digital collages or posters • Create a "Teachable Moments" video teaching the concept to peers • Create an educational game • Create a podcast or video • STEM tasks • Surveys- for example, "survey fifty people, use a graph maker to show results, complete a written or typed report on the findings, and present the information for others using a media platform, such as PowerPoint." (an excellent way to integrate multiple subjects)
Personal, peer, and teacher evaluations following a rubric	**Monitor Progress**	Personal, peer, and teacher evaluations following a rubric

Monitoring Progress

While students are learning, it is necessary to follow up and reiterate expectations. As shown in the above sections, there are many ways to monitor student progress throughout the lesson. Progress monitoring should affirm that students are mastering concepts. On assessments, students should be able to explain concepts in verbal and written formats, such as on standardized test and presentations to parents. In order to do this, make sure the content is deep and not surface level. A quick assessment can be taken daily, midweek, or at the end of the lesson to monitor students' individual progress. Throughout the rest of the year, the tasks can be brought back to the forefront of students' minds to use as they answer questions. Easy peasy lemon squeezy! Now let's look at two more samples of hybrid learning lesson plans.

NOTES

Lesson Plan #3
Math-Understanding Rates, Ratios, and Algebra

By Melanie Wells

Essential Questions: What is the difference between rate and ratio? Is there a relationship between an equation, t-table, and graph?

Objectives:

1. Understand the concept of a ratio and use ratio language to describe the relationship between two quantities.

2. Understand the concept of a unit rate.

3. Use ratio and rate reasoning to solve real-world and mathematical problems by reasoning about tables of ratios, number line diagrams, and equations.

4. Recognize and represent proportional relationships between quantities.

5. Use variables to represent two quantities in a real-world problem that changes in relationship to one another; write an equation to express one quantity, thought of as the dependent variable, in terms of the other quantity, thought of as the independent variable. Analyze the relationship between the dependent and independent variables using equations, t-tables, and graphs.

6. Understand the relationship from two values (x, y), including reading these from a table or a graph.

Learning Targets:

• I can describe the difference between rates and ratios.

• I can describe the relationship between an equation, t-table, and graph.

• I can communicate and demonstrate my conceptual understanding of the following vocabulary words: rates, slope, variables, coefficients, constant, y-intercept.

• I can apply various objectives to solve a multi-step problem with understanding.

Prerequisites:

Students should know how to:

• represent amounts as fractions, decimals, and percent (refer to math lesson plan #1)

• translate expressions and equations

• complete a function table

• plot points on a coordinate grid

Conceptual Understanding for Rates and Ratios: The transition from whole numbers to fractions is important because if students are not comfortable with fractions, they will not be comfortable with rates, ratios, and proportions. Since algebra is based on understanding the relationship between two quantities, a prerequisite to understanding algebra is understanding fractions, rates, ratios, and proportions.

Conceptual Understanding for Algebra to be Reviewed Daily:

1. What is algebra? Algebra is solving for an unknown number.

2. Why do we use algebra? We use algebra when we have a problem that follows a particular pattern. If we recognize the pattern, then we can repeat the pattern to answer various questions about specific situations. Basically, algebra is solving for the unknown.

3. Why is the number unknown? The number is unknown because it can change (vary) based on the person or situation. We use a variable to represent the unknown number.

4. Algebraic equations and expressions represent a pattern. The pattern can be placed on a ttable and then plotted on a coordinate grid. Graphing the information provides a visual representation of the relationship and pattern between two quantities (x and y).

5. Charts and graphs can make it easier to organize and visualize the pattern. Predictions can be made based on the pattern of the data and information.

Lesson Steps:

1.) Introduction: Begin the lesson by asking students to define rate, ratio, and proportion in their own words. Help students understand that all three are similar to fractions because they compare and explain the relationship between two quantities. Use measurement conversions to show how to convert units to introduce unit rate and unit price to answer word problems (such as "what are the miles per hour?). Use online pictures to help students become comfortable with unit rates and discuss common rates: heart rate, miles per hour, amount of gas per gallon, dollars per hour, words per minute, and price per pound.

2.) Discussion: Help students understand that when they are given a scenario (word problem), they can translate it into an equation, organize the data using a t-table, and plot the coordinates on a graph. When the two quantities are placed on a graph, it is easier to see the relationship. One has to be the independent variable, and the other one has to be the dependent variable.

3.) Guided Practice: Guide students through integrated algebra problems (at least three). Help students identify and label the rate, slope, constant, y-intercept, variable, coefficient, and independent/dependent variables. Model how to create an equation, t-table, and graph for each problem to show the connection visually. For each problem, students will write the expression, use a t-table to solve the second part of the problem, and then plot the points on a graph to find the unit rate. Here are some examples:

• Write the expression: A camping site rents boats for $35.00 plus $3.00 per hour. Solve the expression for the cost a family will have to pay if they decide to rent a boat for five hours.

• At Tap's Mail, a package costs $3.25 plus $0.25 per pound to be shipped overnight. What is the total cost Mary will have to pay if she ships an overnight package that weighs 5 pounds?

• Kit's Plumbing charges a one-time fee of $50 for house calls plus $20 per hour for each hour worked. Determine the total charge for a 6-hour house call.

• To rent a limousine, Tim must pay an initial fee of $45 in addition to $12 for every hour he has the limousine reserved. What will be Tim's final bill if he reserves the limousine for 7 hours?

• At a bowling alley, there is a flat fee of $5.00 to rent shoes. In addition, it costs $1.25 for each game bowled. What is the total cost for 8 games?

• A car rental company will rent a car for a flat rate of $32 with an additional charge of $0.60 for each mile driven. What will be the total cost of renting a car for someone driving 20 miles?

4.) Check for Understanding: On an exit card, present students with a word problem and ask them to create a t-table, equation, and graph to answer the problem. Each part should be labeled with the rate (slope), constant, y-intercept, variable, coefficient, and independent/dependent variables.

5.) Integrated Algebra Task: Allow students to work with a partner to create two integrated algebra problems for their peers from another group to complete. Perform a peer check to make sure the other group effectively solved and labeled the problem.

Lesson Plan #4
ELA- Argumentative Writing

By Melanie Wells

Essential Question: Can arguing be productive? Is there a right way to argue:

Objectives:

1. W Standard 1: Write arguments to support claims, distinguish the claim from alternate and opposing claims, and create an organization that establishes clear relationships among claims, counterclaims, reasons, and evidence.

2. RI Standard 1: Quote accurately from a text when explaining what the text says explicitly and when drawing inferences from the text.

3. RI Standard 6: Analyze multiple accounts of the same event or topic noting important similarities and differences in the point of view they represent.

4. RI Standard 8: Delineate and evaluate the argument and specific claim in a text, assessing whether the reasoning is valid, and the evidence i relevant and sufficient; identify false statements and fallacious reasoning

Learning Targets:

• I can write arguments to support claims with clear reasons and relevant evidence.

• I can cite evidence from informational text to support my analysis.

- I can identify aspects of the text that reveal an author's point of view or purpose in an informational text.

- I can identify and evaluate the argument and specific claims in a text.

Conceptual Understanding:

Students should be able to take a reasonable stand on a topic based on research-based information. Allowing students to write their thoughts on paper increases their ability to explain their viewpoints to others in a logical way.

Lesson Steps:

1. Activator (Hook): Ask students to analyze the following quote for 3-5 minutes and write down their thoughts to discuss with a partner.

   Quote: "I see no hope for the future of our people if they are dependent on the irresponsible youth of today, for certainly all youth are reckless beyond words. When I was young, we were taught to be discreet and respectful of elders, but the present youth are exceedingly disrespectful and impatient of restraint."

2. Brief Discussion: After sharing thoughts, let students know this quote was written by Hesiod over 2,000 years ago and discuss new thoughts and feelings about the quote.

3. Introduce: Introduce lesson by telling students they will explore argumentative writing and perception.

4. Essential Questions for the Whole Group Task - Do cell phones cause us to be reckless? Are we paying attention or being disrespectful?

5. Explore: Split students into three or four groups and provide students with digital or paper copies of two articles on cell phones to read and analyze. Students will debate their arguments (in-person, students will discuss using the Fishbowl method, Socratic method, or using a podium to present arguments. Online students will record their arguments, merge them with their peers, and present to the class. Teachers can also have a

virtual meeting with one group at a time and record them to be viewed together as a class).

6. Essential Question for Small Groups: Should parents be allowed to be on social media apps, such as TikTok and Snapchat?

7. Activity: Students will need four articles on social media (or any other relevant topic) to read and analyze. Students will complete a reading carousel with pre-selected group members by rotating to different tables around the room to complete the task.

• The task will be to read the passage on an electronic device or desk and decide how the author is organizing the text. Students will also decide why the author used that text structure.

• Each group member will have a recording sheet of their own and will work together to decide argumentative clues as they prepare for their writings and presentations.

• Students may also find additional research online (be sure to select safe sites and databases for students).

• Once the group decides to agree or disagree, students will individually write an argumentative paragraph or paper with their argument (a rubric should be provided).

8. Check for Understanding: Teacher facilitation and small group discussions

9. Closing Activity: Groups will use an electronic presentation platform to create a final project to present their argument to classmates. This activity should also have a rubric with objectives for citing text evidence, smooth transitions, and persuasive arguments for their views.

All four of the lessons presented were designed to answer the question, "When are we ever going to use this?" Answering this question ensures students will stay engaged and motivated in-person and online. Each lesson step should have the capability to be taught inperson and online. This chapter gives readers an in-depth view of in-person and online lesson steps merged together to create effective hybrid learning lessons. The main goal was to provide multiple examples of engaging activities that can be used at the beginning, middle, and end of lessons. The above lesson plans are not lesson plan templates; instead, they are guides showing the components necessary to successfully create hybrid learning lesson plans. The best benefit of this lesson planning format is that it ensures students can identify, comprehend, analyze, and apply concepts focused on real-world situations. When students develop their own knowledge, it will not matter how any question is presented on an assessment because students will be able to use logic and reasoning to justify their answers. This lesson format provides a way to activate, engage, and motivate students in any environment. Successful learning occurs when students work together to complete a joint mission. Learning in isolation is not learning at all. As educators, we can help our students find their niche by providing them with opportunities to engage with real-world situations. Since we do not know the problems our students will have ten to twenty years from now, we must constantly transform education so our students can become innovators who are willing to apply their knowledge and talents gleaned from the question, "When are we ever going to use this?"

NOTES

CONCLUSION
PAVING THE PATH TO OUR CHILDREN'S FUTURE

"Success is what we do to build ourselves up; significance is what we do to build others up."
~Anonymous

This book was written to explain the what, why, and how of hybrid learning and hybrid learning environments. Teachers often ask how they can be sure students are prepared for assessments. There has to be more to it than active engagement, right? Yes, definitely. The lesson plan strategies provided in this book prepares students for assessments. By focusing on having a strong start, an engaging middle, and a strong ending, one can check to make sure the lesson steps reach high levels of complexity. Lessons should be designed with assessments in mind; nonetheless, knowledge and skill acquisition should still be the focus of each lesson. If I know the assessment will contain abstract content, I should apply Piaget's and Bloom's theories to scaffold my students until they reach the appropriate assessment level.

This book also explains the growth cycles seen in Maslow's Hierarchy of Needs, Piaget's Theory of Cognitive Development, and Bloom's Taxonomy of Cognitive Skills. Developing an awareness of how the brain learns optimizes lesson delivery. By asking the question when will students use what is being taught, educators will immediately start brainstorming and researching "outside the box" ideas. Our focus in class should be making sure students are safe as we provide opportunities for them to actively engage, innovate, and think critically while establishing a sense of love and belonging. Hopefully, this book adequately explained hybrid learning environments and how to rethink education. As we pave the path for our students, we must continue to be brave and remember passion inspires. This book is a guide to navigate hybrid learning and hybrid learning environments effectively. I hope it provides encouragement and insight as we use this leverage point to maximize learning for all students in every environment.

> *"It is not what you look at that matters, it's what you see."*
> **~Henry David Thoreau**

What do you see? I see a young woman. Yet, I also see the older woman. Let's always strive to help our students see the best. After reading this book, I hope you feel confident about heading into the school year.

Oh yeah, you know how I was able to break down the steps of driving into the simplest form, and we just finished breaking down hybrid learning into its simplest form? Quantum Physics is the science and study of matter in its simplest form. See, easy peasy! Throughout my years of teaching, I have realized my purpose in life is to help others find theirs. I wish you the best of luck as you prepare your students for greatness. Thank you.

REFERENCES

Emmons, M. Key Statistics about Millennials in the Workplace.
https://dynamicsignal.com/2018/10/09/key-statistics-millennials-in-the-workplace/.

Jensen, E. (2010). Teaching with poverty in mind: what being poor does to kids' brains and what schools can do about it. ASCD.

Sinek, S. (2019). Start with why: how great leaders inspire everyone to take action. Penguin Business.

ABOUT THE AUTHOR

Assistant principal and educational speaker Melanie Wells is a transformative leader with over 15 years as an educator. Her post-compulsory educational training includes Jackson State University (bachelor's degree), Mississippi College (master's and specialist degrees), and The University of Mississippi (Specialist in Ed. Leadership). She has teaching and administrative experience in both title and non-title schools at the elementary and secondary levels. Her areas of expertise include brain-based research, student engagement, and intrinsic motivation.

⊕ wellsconnectingdots.org
🔲 melanie-wells-9444b437
🔲 melanie.wells.52
🔲 principalwells1
✉ wellsmelanie47@gmail.com